*Copyright © 2023 Elizabeth Langlois
All rights reserved.*

Cover art by Nicolas Langlois

Believe the truth about yourself no matter how beautiful it is.

Macrina Wiederkehr

> **Unwritten Poetry** *
>
> Nothing satisfies when poetry is denied.
> Nothing but the bloody dawn,
> The purple pink of nature's ink
> Spread across the liquid lake.
> Nothing but our meeting eyes,
> When love is not disguised
> But boldly painted on your face
> And felt in your warm embrace.
>
> — Elizabeth Langlois 6/2/08

* Refer to page 103 for poem

Dedication

This book is dedicated to our incredible mom who passed away on Thanksgiving night, 2021. She gave us the best gift a mother can give which is to love unconditionally and she extended that love to the world. She was and is an inspiration to us all.

With love,
Ann, Aimee, Steve, Bob, Tom, Paul and Jennie

Prologue 11
    Still Life 11
    Friends 12

Poems From My Forties 13
    North Shore Song in Three Parts 14
    Personal Reflection for Tom 15
    Friendship 16
    I Love 17
    Mask 17
    Colored Words 18
    Gifts 18
    Two verses for Bobbi 19
    Calvary 20
    Acceptance 20
    Easter Morn 21
    Offering 22
    Loneliness 22
    Poverty Prayer 23
    To God 23
    Teach Me to Love 24
    To Kay 24
    Together 25
    Litany of Praise 26
    Of My Father 26
    Winter Words 27
    Solitude 28
    Contemplation 29
    There is My Love 29
    God's Will is Love 30
    The Seamless Robe 31
    Dialogue 32
    Offertory 32
    Reality 33
    Priest's Portrait 33
    Witness 34
    Communion 35
    Conversation with Jesus 35
    Passiontime 36
    Decision 36
    Shoe Story 37
    To Annie 37

Poems From My Fifties **39**
    Three Quarter Time 40
    Eden 40
    Questions and Answers 41
    Blessing 41
    Ash Wednesday 42
    Autumn Coat 43
    Be Still 43
    Birthday Blessing 44
    Enough 44
    Little Lanterns 45
    Reflection 45
    Homecoming 45
    Baptism 46
    Bittersweet 47
    Advent 48
    March Came In 49
    Holy Ground 50
    Forever 51
    Without You 51
    First and Last 52
    Listen 53
    Advent 54
    Morning Mist 57
    Evensong 57
    To an Autumn God 58
    Silence is Golden 58
    Here Comes My Bride 59
    Visitation 60
    Presence 61
    Sisters Prayer 62
    To Be 63
    Rain, Rain 64
    Fecundity 64
    The Visit 65
    Adoration 66
    Soldiers Field 67
    The Lilies 68
    Waiting in May 70
    Heartbroken 70
    Unveiling 71
    Friends Dialogue 71

Joyce Kilmer Revisited 72
Waves 72
Life Goes On 73
Yes to No 73
Sister Moon 74
Home 74
Come Back 75
Remember the Times 76
Free Verse 77

Poems From My Sixties 79

    Garden 80
    Kataluma 81
    When you are gone 81
    Twins 82
    Underground 82
    Dare 83
    Pecos River Reflection 83
    Grief 84
    Here and Now 84
    Samaritan Woman 85
    Mandorla* 86
    Silence 86
    The Storm 87
    To John 87
    Prayer While Watching the Ice Go Out 87
    Eve of Pentecost 88
    Dawn 88
    Olympic Opening 1996 89
    Winter 89
    Canticle 90
    Words 91
    Common Ground 91
    Going to Kosovo 92
    Mountain Place 92
    Question 93
    And I Was Loved 93
    Surprise Visit 93
    Open Eye Meditation 94
    March Madness 95
    Eagles 95
    TRILOGY ON GRIEF .... **Error! Bookmark not defined.**

    Skygrief 96
    Mornings' Sunrise 96
    Lost and Found 96

Poems From My Seventies 97
    Thou 98
    70th Birthday Thoughts 98
    Mary of Magdala 99
    The Poems 99
    Lectio Divine 100
    Initiation 100
    Wild Child 101
    Christmas Message 102
    Love Signs 102
    Mother God 103
    Unwritten Poetry 103
    Heart Space 103
    Everything Belongs 104
    To Peggy Thompson 105
    Palm Sunday 105
    North Shore Morning 106
    106
    Dawn with Psalm 19 at Ravenrest* 107
    Easter 2012 107

Poems from my Eighties 109
    At the Monastery 110
    110
    Winter Rest 111
    Now 112
    Blessed 113
    .... **Error! Bookmark not defined.**

About the Author 115

Prologue

Still Life

I have decided to let you know about my personality through the image of a still life portrait. I would like to paint a picture of myself with words. I hope it will help you to know me better and understand my personality. In painting a picture of myself with my words, I would want you to imagine a brightly colored still life portrait of fruit, flowers and a translucent, very fragile alabaster jar. The shadows in this picture are essential-they bring out the light and are integral to healing. Anyone who looks at the still life will know who I am. This portrait could never be in black and white for God has clothed me in a coat of many colors.

The flowers speak of my childhood, especially of my father who surrounded me with them, taught me the names and lovingly nurtured them from seed to full bloom- as he did me. The flowers also reflect the way I have opened up over the years- a slow and sometimes painful process that reminds me of what Jesus said in John 12:24 "Very truly I tell you, unless I give of what falls into the earth and dies it remains just a single grave but if it dies it bears much fruit". All of the flowers in this picture are wildflowers, somewhat uncomfortable because they have been taken out of their natural habitat and have been forced into a vase, I see my favorite forget me-nots who grow by the water and remind me of the north shore, my favorite place. Gold and black-eyed Susan's (my father always said when he saw them by the road "summer is almost over."), shy violets hiding under leaves in the shade, white daisies (he loves me, he loves me not), and lastly the pink wild rose (my middle name) so fragrant and delicate, so vulnerable but don't forget the hidden thorns on their stems!! Some are tightly braided and others fully open to the sun, the rain, the snow and the stars. All of these flowers speak to the beauty in variety and the importance of just being and of trust. Jesus said, "see how the lilies of the field are clothed, they never toil or spin but Solomon in all his glory was not arrayed as one of them".

The fruit reminds me of fertility and the many people who have helped me grow, have nurtured and challenged me, they speak to me of the love joy and patience, kindness, generosity, faithfulness and self-control that are VERY slowly becoming a part of who I am. The wide variety helps me to connect with how complicated I am and yet they also remind me of the simple pleasure they give me as I enjoy eating them or just looking at them. They speak to me of satisfaction, delight and the fullness of time. They also speak to me of my seven beautiful children and my grandchildren.

The alabaster jar is a symbol of my feminine nature, a container of being. It has tiny cracks all over it and one large break that has been mended. It was almost completely broken in two but was lovingly put back together with the help of God and the friends God has placed in my life. It speaks to me of my fragility, brokenness and that I need others. It tells me that I am independent. I am like the alabaster jar filled with expensive perfume which Mary of Bethany broke and then used to anoint the feet of Jesus, wiping his feet with her hair. It reminds me that I am called to be broken and then poured out in service of others. I celebrate this in a poem I wrote entitled "friends".

Friends

After you have washed my feet with your tears
After you have broken the jar of your fears
After you have dried my feet with your hair
After you have kissed them naked and bare
Then I will break my hearts disguise
And kiss them with my gentle eyes
And pour perfume that never ends
From the alabaster jar named friends

1
Poems From My Forties

North Shore Song in Three Parts

I watched the campfire burning bright
Reflected in the eyes of those I love.
Children singing songs of joy,
Flowers around the flame.
Then suddenly I knew
The "Word made Flesh" was part of this
They are not ours but His.
God will carry on for us
As we pray and learn to trust.

I watched the campfire burning bright,
The tongues of fire speak to me -
We are like the way you love.
Leaping high in orange and red
Casting light beyond,
Until we're not fed by the Word,
Shared and lived.
Then we fade, we starve, grow cold
Until we're dead.

I watched the campfire burning low
The flames all blue, a tiny glow.
We left the little circle of light
And stepped into the blackest night
Fingers touching and entwined
Like the branches of a vine.
We follow Christ, eternal flame,
As we each are called by name.
Then share the night turned into day
Lighting each other along the way.

Dedicated to my children and grandchildren who have been lighting my way and have taught me how to love.

Personal Reflection for Tom

I'm crying my love,
My tears are a prayer.
You gave me a gift,
But I was not there.

The gift is your love,
I have blocked it all out,
Just saying the words
But feeling the doubt.

Please try to forgive,
The tears are for real,
So is the prayer
And the love I now feel.

I want to start now
To be really me,
And give you a gift
My love deep and free.

May 1973
Marriage Encounter

Friendship

Friendship is a waiting game -
We play between each other.
I wait for you and you for me,
Afraid of what we'll discover.

Friendship is a lonely game -
We meet, we love and share.
Then know that soon we'll be apart,
And that is hard to bear.

Friendship is a risky game -
I tell you how I feel.
Then trust you to confide in me,
And reveal how you are real.

Friendship is a fearsome game -
We play with this in mind.
It's scary when I think you'll laugh,
At what I know you'll find.

Friendship is a trusting game -
To love is to reveal.
How you are you and I am me,
Accepting what we feel.

Friendship is a faithful game -
I believe in what you say.
Then trust that you will seek me out,
That truth will be our way.

Friendship is a lovely game -
To play it makes us know.
That when we seek each other out,
We'll meet to talk and grow.

So be my friend and I'll be yours -
We won't be playing games.
When I love you and you love me
We'll never be the same.

November 1973

I Love

I love your hands
So lean and strong and warm.
They hold mine clasped round
Your strength in them I've found.

I love your face
It shines like burnished gold
Or silver polished bright
It sheds a lovely light.

I love your eyes
They smile like sun on snow
Or moon upon a lake
I like the love they make.

December 1973
Dedicated to my dear husband Tom on our 30th Wedding Anniversary –
May 11, 1987

Mask

I had a mask and wore it well.
It felt just right, people did not stare.
It covered every part of what was really me,
I forgot who was hiding under there.

Christ said, "Love one another as yourself",
What is love and where?
My mask was getting tight.
I tried to take it off.
I pulled and tugged all by myself,
Then gave up in despair.

Christ sent his friends to be mine too.
They loved and told me so.
I know my mask was falling off.
I cried and let it go.

December 1973
One of my earliest poems

Colored Words

I need new words for love
New letters put together on a page.
Black and white I cannot use.
I'll take the children's colored pens
And sketch a word that never ends.
Begin with purple, red and blue,
Bright and sad together.
Red for warmth,
Blue to say, "It cannot be".
I'll paint new words for you –
Wild splashes on the canvas.
When you see the purple say
"I'm glad she loves me and colors me free".

December 1973

Gifts

A gift was given, wrapped in cloth,
Torn strips from Mary's gown.
Her Joseph helped to tear the bands,
Then wrapped them round and round.
She listened to the baby's cry and
Fed him at her breast.
Then laid him down to watch him sleep
Before she tried to rest.

A gift was given to the world,
A world that knew him not.
The Word made human grew in love,
To forgive as He forgot.
His parents had to give him up –
They gave their son away.
The love they taught had set him free,
They knew he could not stay.

A gift was given, stripped and hung,
Again, they bound him round.
Then laid him in a stony cave,
A corpse upon the ground.
The women came as dawn grew bright
And filled the Easter sky
The bands of cloth limp in the tomb
Proclaimed a resurrection cry.

Now we are gifts, Christ sets us free
From bands that bind us tight.
We must give our Christmas gifts
Our words and deeds of light.
So please accept me as I am
And I will try to give
The gift of me accepting you
And love you as Jesus does.

Written November 1973
Dedicated to Andre Holt in 2012

Two Verses for Bobbi

If I bind you to myself it is not love.
Love demands freedom to choose,
Air to breathe and space to run,
The dark of night and blazing sun.

If I bind you to myself it is not love.
I kill love demanding yours.
Me, passed round, brings death,
Love choked of its last breath.

December 1973

Calvary

Why this year God are you forcing me to look;
Before I just read your Passion from the book?

Why this year God do you make me turn my head;
To gaze on your face and see that you are dead?

Why this year God do you seize my hand to feel;
The wounds of nail and sword to know that they are real?

Why this year God do you open wide my ears?
I hear you say "It's finished" just as the end draws near.

Why this year God? The reasons are clear to me,
You want me to experience the Paschal Mystery.

Acceptance

I never had a friend –
It was so easy
Just to hide behind a smile,
Afraid of letting go.
There was no room for anyone,
I was so full of me.
I did not even know I was alone.
To know meant I had known love
And longed for someone so.
How could I miss something
I had never known.

I never knew a friend –
Someone who let me fly
Without a string.
Who just stood by with arms outstretched
Until I chose to land, a wounded bird
Who loved without a word.

I never loved a friend –
Until I met my God
Whose gaze did not demand my love;
Whose arms a tree spread wide.
I wanted to be caught in them
And rest upon the limbs;
To die to self a bit each day
Until becoming stripped of me.
I too, could become a tree.

March 1974

Easter Morn

I watched the eastern sky
On a cloudy Easter morn.
The sun was hidden from my sight
No sign of living grace.
Then saw a brighter light
In the eyes of a patient's face.

I watched the eastern sky
On a gloomy Easter morn.
Where was the glowing golden dawn
That helped me to know he lived?
I felt it in my husband's hand,
Reaching to forgive.

I watched the eastern sky
On a chilly Easter morn.
Where was the warmth of other years
Pushing buds from dark to light?
I found it in the children's arms,
Hugging me so tight.

I watched the eastern sky
On a darkened Easter morn.
Then knew that Christ had conquered death.
His people are the golden glow of dawn.
I heard Him in their Alleluia Song!

April 1974

Offering

Between the moon and stars
We stood to say goodbye
The moon a silver sliver high
The stars like the glistening tears I cried.

Between the dark and dawn
I lay so quiet and still
Remembering the space you fill,
It is so difficult to do God's will.

Between my God and me
The feelings for you stay.
I know my love won't go away
So give it to the Lord each day.

May 1974

Loneliness

I am so lonely when you speak the words
You think I need to hear.
Instead of the truth a lie,
Pretty sounds that make me cry.

I am so lonely when our eyes just meet
And gaze is not held long.
My love is spoken there
And fills the space we cannot share.

I am so lonely when we touch, your hand in mine,
Then only say "good-bye".
As if we are afraid
To love the love for which we're made.

I am so lonely but not alone, I love,
And know that loving is not wrong.
That loneliness embraced
Finds Christ beneath its empty face.

July 1974

Poverty Prayer

Make me poor –Your riches cover me.
Help me to sit upon your shore.
To listen as I seek your depth
Until I cease to breathe, begin my death.

Make me poor –Your love is wealth enough.
I know how weak I am.
Teach me to walk across your lake;
When I fall your hand my hand will take.

Make me poor –Reduce my I to you.
I always want to live for me.
Help me to stand upon your shore;
Seeking your will, asking no more.

August 1974

To God

I thought I'd meet you in the woods -
Beneath a shady tree.
Instead, my soul was desert bound
And in the heat your will I found.

I thought I'd meet you in the woods -
We'd walk and watch the birds.
Instead, I found you in the dark
Then in the night I heard a lark.

I thought I'd meet you in the woods –
So cool and green with ferns.
Instead, I found you in the dust
And learned again just how to trust.

I thought I'd meet you in the woods –
We'd talk and watch the moon.
Instead, I walked the starless night
And found that people were my light.

September 1974

Teach Me to Love

Teach me to love – I don't know what it is.
I only know that what I thought love was - is wrong,
And that I cannot give or take when lovers come along.

Teach me to love – it is so scary and I'm afraid.
I've been so full of me and not of you.
I know that you are always there
but I am closed to you and all you've shared.

Teach me to love – the school will have no desk,
The blackboard used will be my heart.
The classes held each day.
Christ the teacher of His way.

Teach me to love – the way of cross and crown.
In daily chores and children's quarrels,
Meals to cook, washing pot and dish.
I want to learn that love
Is saying "yes" to this.

To Kay

Like Mary, you're my Mother,
Like Mary, carry Christ.
You bring Him forth to give to me
As I fight from death to life.

Like Mary, you're my Mother,
Like Mary, Wisdom's Crown.
You teach me to be willing,
To be willing to be found.

Like Mary, you're my Mother,
You accept me as I am.
But challenge me to become
Meek and humble as a lamb.

Like Mary, you're my Mother,
Like Mary, set Christ free.
To grow in truth and beauty
And love Him by loving me.

Like Mary, you're my Mother,
My God gave you to me.
You show me how to "clean my cup"
And follow from birth to free.

Like Mary, watched her Son
And saw Him die and rise,
You help me to die to selfishness,
Speak truth instead of lies.

Thank you, Spiritual Mother,
Thank you, God above.
Help me to follow my Brother
As I grow in the Spirit of Love.

Dedicated to Kay VanKampen, my spiritual director and mentor.

Together

We are now together in our separateness,
Undemanding and renounced,
Emptied from despair – still alone,
Always letting go, never seeking to control.

We are now together in our love for God
Who calls us each in different ways.
To walk the same deserted path
Following Jesus, our brother who is love and lover.

We will be together in eternity.
Forever friends, unbound from time.
One in love, intercourse divine.
Perfect joy we long for you
But wait until our walk is through.

Litany of Praise

I praise God for distress,
I praise God for my pain.
I praise God for the times
My tears flow like the rain.

I praise God for the cross,
I praise God for Jesus 'death.
I praise God for forgiving
As He uttered His last breath.

I praise God for Mother Mary,
I praise God for her Son.
I praise God for the Spirit
Who makes them three in one.

I praise God for the servants,
I praise God for their love.
Fruit of the Holy Spirit
Sent from heaven above.

Of My Father

I saw peonies today.
All the memories came back
Of my Father.

He was a flower man.
They were his dearest friends -
I was too.

He taught me to love every bloom
And how to call them by name –
So, I did.

He started them early in March
From seeds sown in flats filled with earth.
And they grew.

We watched as they burst from the soil,
Like a child beginning its birth
Spring began.

I remember him tending his flowers
And loving them so they would grow –
Just like me.

He died the year I was seventeen
The winter was just beginning -
In my heart.

I'm glad winter only lasts 'til spring
Seventeen was too young for me to die –
I agreed.

Now, when I see other flower gardens,
He speaks to me in each bloom and says,
Remember.

Winter Words

Today I looked outside and saw the autumn gone.
My tree, the one I see when lying in bed
Had lost its yellow dress.
The wind played winters song
Naked branches etched against the sky, Black on gray.
On the ground the leaves turned brown
And withered where they lay.
A storm had stripped them overnight
And swept away their golden light.

Today I know that winter had been born.
A tiny flake of snow melted on the dirt still warm.
The other seasons stir my heart
But winter seldom does its part.
Then "The Word" spoke in a silent shout,
"My steps are easier to know
When you follow me through the snow."

Solitude

I like to know you want to be alone.
Sometimes the urge to get away from people
Overcomes me.
I understand that we need each other.
But when this time is over I just need me
To sit alone and be.

I want right now to sit by myself.
To hear the silence of a star filled night,
Or listen to the thunder and the rain.
To know I don't have to give
Until I'm full again.

I think of Christ and how He sought solitude.
The press of crowds was so demanding –
He got into a boat.
The lake was calm, a mirrored sea,
A single bird was flying free.

I know he had to be alone,
Away from the crowds, to pray.
His Father – friend wanted just to hear from Him.
He left and stole away.

People who need people
Also need to be apart; to sit alone and still,
To find again their eternal friend.

Contemplation

Burn pure fire of light, your flower from red to white.
Consume the sin inside my passions and my pride.
My greed and sloth and hate of me,
My gluttony and jealousy.

Burn pure fire of light, your flame my soul ignites.
The outer skin where pain is felt,
impurities your heat will melt,
Until inside we will combine
As one – your will is mine.

Burn pure fire of light, divine delight as we unite.
The union of your Spirit, my soul –
Abandonment to God's control.
Perfect lovers we are led to
Where God has made our marriage bed.

April 1975

There is My Love

There is my love – see Him in the crib crying for
His Mother's milk. Helpless, weak, infant God,
So meek.

There is my love – see Him teaching teachers,
Doing God's work; going home, obeying, growing,
Knowing love, feeling love.
Love being loved and loving.

There is my love – see Him walking on the
Desert sand. Tall, strong and tan. Muscled arms
And large brown hands.
Hair sun streaked, blowing free,
Eyes so deep they see eternity.

There is my love – see Him talking to the people.
The desert made His heart a cell, ready now
To give His love away, to make the sick one well.
Being love and speaking love.
His neighbors called Him mad and so He was -
Obsessed with living,
Possessed with giving.

There is my love – see Him on the cross.
I don't want to look at Him – He was so beautiful unbroken.
The nails slide through without a sound.
His blood pours silently from sword split side.
How can silence be so loud?
His love is spent, the reed is bent.
They lift Him up, his eyes meet mine,
Forgiveness in a glance. His look my lance.

There is my love – see Him after dawn, cooking
By the lake. I sit with Him, my hand
He takes and whispers in my ear,
"I love you, dear, come walk with me,
I'll show you where I live.
We'll laugh and talk and share,
Then spend the night in prayer.
As you climb your hill to do God's will
Gethsemane is ours.
Remember me and this
Tomorrow once again our eyes will kiss
And we will gather flowers."
August 1975

God's Will is Love

God's will is love, a love I do not
Understand and God wants me to accept.
I can never reason out this will.
It is not reasonable – love never is.

When God gave Jesus to us, God knew
That the only way Jesus could be given
Back was by allowing Him to choose.
This choice of death so necessary to rebirth
Is one of many paradoxes in living a spiritual life.
We are asked to make the same choice.

This is God's will. God's will is love.
Why did I think I could love with my mind?
Concepts and ideas are useful only when they
Come from a softened heart,
A broken heart, a heart of flesh.
Love can only flow from there.

And so we learn who our brother Jesus is
And do what He did, making choices until
Our will becomes the same as God's.
Many times the only action God asks of us is to wait.
How humbling to wait for our Beloved,
What action in surrender and acceptance.
God's will is always love – God is love.

The Seamless Robe

Jesus, help me to be naked in front of you.
Please strip me as the soldiers did you.
There is nothing I can do that you have not already done,
Except in sin I have been clothed
And you were dressed in seamless robe.

Black velvet was the cloth I had
Until you looked into my eyes
And then it became a veiled disguise.
I looked and turned away,
Then looked again and knew you'd not betray.

Help me now to see the selfish me,
To know that it was I who sent you off to die.
My death can never be as yours.
I, the blemished lamb stand waiting for your hand.
You have made me ready to come back home.
Only you can tear my veil today
And give your seamless robe away.

September 1975

Dialogue

Jesus: "Accept the nails of doubt and fear, I
Felt forsaken too. Once driven in your
Upturned hands, new life I'll give to you."

Elizabeth: "I will hope, even in my despair, along
The cross-path. My little wood is light to
Bear because before me you were there."

Jesus: "On the cross my cup o'er flowed,
Blood spilled on the ground – everlasting
Covering for the sinner found."

Elizabeth: "My dying has begun, bloodless
Death for love. God my executioner sends
Down the Spirit – Dove."

March 1976

Offertory

From our mothers hiding place God called
Us each by name and pledged our truth
In timelessness before the world was made.

The day we wed and spoke the words of covenant
And faith meant more today because we live
Those promises by God's grace.

I praise and thank our loving God who
Has made us one because we both are
Willing to follow Jesus Christ, the Son.

God speaks to me today and asks me
Now to give my love away. I gladly,
Freely offer you to Jesus on this day.

O Holy Spirit, bless this man whom you
Have given to me.
Anoint Him now with your sweet love
That others may be freed.

April 1976
To my husband Tom on his ordination

Reality

Make me real God -
I need to be human.
So little in my life has penetrated.
Hard-core stuff my heart.
"Help", my only sound,
Crying as I drown.

Make me real God –
I need to be touched.
To know that I am as good as you have made me.
Sin, like seven veils
Binds tight my flesh from view,
I hide from all but you.

Make me real God –
I need to be healed.
Pretending is a game I have played all my life.
I'm tired of the rules.
Break me like the humpty-man,
Put me back together again.

June 1976

Priest's Portrait
It is not until we are human that we become divine

This is not an abstract, your embrace of all for one.
You paint a realistic scene this noon,
The wheat is ground, we gather round,
Your broken body hugs a tree,
Picture hung for all to see.
Die again another day so others can go out to play.

This is not an abstract, your embrace of all for one.
You draw, clear lines, colors bright and bold,
Resurrection gold.
One passion for another lived instead for others.
This is your body given for me.
Jesus Christ is all I see.
Live again another day so others can go out to play.
(it is not until we are divine that we become human)

November 1976
Dedicated to Steve LaCanne

Witness
A meditation on Charles de Foucauld

I have been desert bound,
The poorest among the poor.
I speak of being here
Silent sounds of love.
I bring my God whose voice is heard
Without a single spoken word.

I have been desert bound,
The poorest among the poor.
My hut oasis, not mirage.
Come drink and stay with me.
You are my love whose voice is heard
Without a single spoken word.

I have been desert found,
The richest among the rich.
Here is my body broken for you,
Here, the cup to drink.
I am your God whose voice is heard
Without a single spoken word.

February 1977

Communion

    I'm so glad some times are never lost -
    And always can be found.
    Stored tight in covered mind,
    Closed from light and air; foodless fare.

    I'm so glad some times are never lost –
    Dipping oar in clear lake make.
    Ripples like the watered silk
    On ribboned child's curls; silent world.

    I'm so glad some times are never lost –
    Memory forever set.
    In sunset gold and red,
    The night was born anew in our view.

    I'm so glad some times are never lost –
    The birds sing evensong.
    Like stars our love will ever be
    Hidden in the light; Friendship bright.

                                 August 1977

Conversation with Jesus
Two Little Love Poems

    Elizabeth to Jesus:
        "Your smile breaks across my sky
        Like lightening. Pounding, clapping
        In my heart like thunder. Someday
        Your smile will strike me dead
        And I will live in your thunder beat forever."

    Jesus to Elizabeth:
        "Your eyes are naked, do not
        Cover them or be ashamed. I can
        See all of me in them and touch
        You with my gaze. Their loveliness
        Never ceases to amaze."

Passiontime

I cry when you hold my hand.
Your touch destroys
The silent noise.

I know that God is making out of me
An earthen pot.
I weep a lot.

I cry when your eyes touch mine.
I see the pain
That softly reigns.

I know that God is making out of me
A fragile dish.
What is Her wish?

I cry when you turn around
And walk away.
Why can't you stay?

I know that you are making out of me
A shattered plate,
Broken, I wait.

March 1978

Decision

Yes God, I want to walk again
On your passion path of love.
I was sitting on the shore
Losing you, refusing you.

Yes God, I want to walk again
Across the moon pathed lake.
I was resting on the shore
Losing you, refusing you.

Yes God, I want to walk again,
Each step is fiat filled.
My eyes are fixed upon your tree.
Reminding me, finding me.

July 1978

Shoe Story

My memories lay dusty on the closet floor.
Old shoes I had forgotten long ago.
I opened the door and put them
On my mind.
They spoke of times I had forgotten.
I cried and walked the pain-path.
One day the shoemaker came and touched
My blistered brain.
"How beautiful the feet of those who
Bring good news.
I spoke to them who came unshod;
I gave them shoes to wear."
Last time I looked my closet floor was bare but
Jesus Christ was standing there.

September 1979

To Annie

You are a bride today -
What God has given I give away,
Another time I heard your cry.
My heartbeat to the music of "just born",
My blood a blanket for your tiny form,
Your lifeline cord was cut.
Set free to be
My first child – girl named Ann Marie.

You are a bride today –
What God has given I give away.
I will be the music maker now,
Your words will dry my tears.
"I do, I will, I choose to love you dear."
Now I will cut the cord
That sets you free.
My first child – woman, Ann Marie.

June 1979
Dedicated to my daughter Ann Marie

2
Poems From My Fifties

Three Quarter Time

I sit midway between the tops of trees and ground;
A little more above the middle than below.
It is three-quarter time for me.
I am glad and sad.
Glad to know that I have passed the point of no return,
Sad so many minutes past have slipped away unnoticed,
So many times not cherished.
I relish more the now and let the half be past.
I want to dance the Waltz today
So let three-quarter music play.

May 1984
Written on Father Jim's deck at his cabin

Eden

The trees are praying in the wind,
The birds sing morning song.
The colors of the sky and lake,
A blue that only God can make.

An Eden here and I am Eve,
Walking naked in the woods.
No shame is mine, no doubt or fears,
The rising sun has dried my tears.

I am clothed with a garment white,
God's seamless robe of love.
On my finger is a ring,
I am betrothed to a King.

This Eden is the Kingdom come,
This Eve my Adam found.
In our garden we can rest,
Our union has been Godly blessed.

July 1984

Questions and Answers

How do I open the gate?
I know you stand and knock.
How do I open the gate?
The one without a lock?

How do I open my heart
To let your love come in?
How do I open my heart
So hard and full of sin?

Be quiet and let me speak
My words will open the gate.
Be still and know my voice,
I stand at the door and wait.

Let the feelings touch your heart
You are my own desire.
I have created you from the start
And set your heart on fire.

July 1984

Blessing

I am beginning to see myself as blessing,
Not curse, a child of the Universe.
I am beginning to see myself as God's design,
Made so from the beginning of time.

If all would know themselves as blessed,
As joy, delight and grace.
Then the earth would be restored
And we would call it Eden – Place.

May 1985

Ash Wednesday

Throw me on the wheel God
Throw me on the wheel.
Take me and remake me
Break my heart of steel.

Center me in you God
Center me in you.
Take me and remake me
Fashion me anew.

Mold this lump of clay God
Mold this lump of clay.
Take me and remake me.
In your hands I lay.

I want to be your vase God
I want to be your vase.
Take me and remake me
I long to see your face.

I want to be your plate God
I want to be your plate.
Take me and remake me
I am yours to re-create.

Ash Wednesday, 1986

Autumn Coat

Autumn world your many-colored coat is back;
Your red, your orange, your golden yellow haze.
The trees burn like the colors of a blaze;
Short fire of fall dies quickly as I gaze.

Autumn world your many-colored coat is back;
My heart leaps to your fabric turning bright.
So short the flaming glory in my sight;
That as I turn you change to winter white.

October 1985

Be Still

Be still and know that I am God.

The trees are still, they do not move their leaves or branch but wait
For spirit-wind to let them dance.

The birds are still, they do not move their wings but wait,
Like trees, to hear the song that they will sing.

The lake is still and looking in its face
I see the birds and trees created by God's grace.

My friends, be still and let me give you song and dance.
Look into the water of your souls and see your face in mine –

It is divine.

July 1985

Birthday Blessing

The sun rising o'er Superior lake
Lights my frozen birthday cake.
In the brilliant morning light,
I see the candles burning bright.

I watched the morning rise,
A birthday of surprise.
Stars still shining fade from view,
As the day is born anew.

I watched the morning rise,
Awakening my sleepy eyes.
God groans in agony of birth,
It is another day on earth.

I watched the morning rise,
Genesis without disguise.
Another year begins again,
To life and love I say "Amen"!

March 1986
I wrote this on the shore of Lake Superior on my 53rd birthday

Enough

The table's set,
The cup, the plate.
Come in, my love
Our supper waits.
This vintage is the one I saved
This bread the loaf I raised.

The table's set,
The plate, the cup.
Come in, my love,
I'll fill you up.
My bread, my wine, my love divine,
I name them all Enough.

June 1987
One of my favorite poems. John Parkos memorized it and used it in his homily for Deacon Ted Diedrich's funeral.

Little Lanterns

Little lanterns of the night
Flickering off and on your lights
Being what you're made to be
Sparkling in the night for me

I want to be a firefly too
I want to light the dark for you
I want to be a beacon bright
A little lantern of the night

June 1986

Reflection

The common tasks of love
The common work
The common life laid down
Because you want them to know
God, who is beauty and truth
And all that is good
Is uncommon

June 1987

Homecoming

O little child within
Come out and play with me.
Come out and be my partner
We'll slide and climb a tree.

O little child within
Why can't you be my friend?
You look so sad and frightened –
So old, so tired and bent.

O little child within
Come, let me take your hand.
Let me walk beside you
Into the enchanted land.

O little child within
I want to give you life.
I want to hear you laughing
I want to hug you tight.

O little child within
I've come to set you free.
I've come to be your midwife
To birth the child in me.

O little child within
I'll let you out to play.
Now we can laugh, and we can sing
And dance the night away.

October 1987
At Villa Maria

Baptism

Launch my thoughts in waves of you
And put them to the test.
Plunge them in the sinner's sea
Then bring them up confessed.

Launch my will in waves of you
Break o'er my bow the wine.
I want to float and let you be
The captain of my mind.

Launch my flesh in waves of you,
My little boat of bread.
That you may drown the "self of me"
And raise me from the dead.

Launch my heart in waves of you,
Let the pounding cease.
Nor let my ship be put to shore
Once christened and released.

August 1987
Written on the North Shore down on the beach.
Lake Superior is very sacred to me and is one of my muses.

Bittersweet

    Jesus, you are bittersweet,
    Your cross is now a plate.
    A wooden dish you lie upon,
    As silently you wait.

    Jesus, you are bittersweet,
    Wrapped in a linen shroud.
    I cannot see your body,
    The cloth is all around.

    Jesus, you are bittersweet,
    The branch curves round your form.
    The little fruit is hanging,
    Bright flowers split and torn.

    Jesus, you are bittersweet,
    But I know you're alive.
    I see the candles burning,
    In your disciples' eyes.

October 1987
Written while reflecting on the altar set up in the chapel at Villa Maria

Advent

Come Lord Jesus
Be our guide.
Gently lead us
Unto your side.

Come Lord Jesus
Be our host.
You welcome us
Who love you most.

Come Lord Jesus
Be our friend.
In communion,
Until the end.

Come Lord Jesus
Be our guest.
We place our heads
Upon your breast.

December 1987

March Came In

March came in like a lamb this year
And played upon the lawn.
She threw away the snow today
Then danced from dusk to dawn.

March came in like a lamb this year
And blew the cold away.
She shines by night in the moon's bright light
And in the sun by day.

March came in like a lamb this year
Now listen to her bleat.
She sings along with birds in song
And children on the street.

March came in like a lamb this year
And like a lion too.
The wind was strong but we were calm,
For we're the chosen few.

March came in like a lamb this year
And climbed a wooden tree.
He spread his limbs as noon turned dim
And brought us all home free.

March 1988
Dedicated to Marv Jacoby and Joe Rowan

Holy Ground

God, make me holy ground,
Plow me round and round.

Turn over my hard upper soil,
I give you permission to toil.

I don't want to be shallow,
I don't want to be fallow.

I'm ready for your blade,
I'm waiting for your spade.

Send the pelting rain
To soak my deepest pain.

Send the blowing wind
To dry the tears within.

Let your seed penetrate rich soil –
Ready to receive.

Let your seed penetrate fertile dirt –
Open to believe.

Let your seed die in the womb of my earth –
When you give birth.

Let your seed become a burning tree –
On fire for thee.

God, make me holy ground
Where only precious pearls are found.

Forever

Let this moment last forever,
Let the clock be set.
Let the hands be gently folded,
Let the face be rest.

Let the moment last forever,
Let the time stand fast.
Let the chimes cease their ringing
Let the half be past.

Let this moment last forever,
Let the ticking cease.
Let the pendulum be stopped,
Let the springs release.

May 1988

Without You

I do not know your loneliness –
Only mine.
I hear it in the music
Still unsung
And in the beating
Of my drum.
This heart pierced through and through
Without you.

April 1988

First and Last

    You are my first love
    You kissed my eyes
    You saw the loneliness
    And heard my cries

    You are my first love
    You kissed my mouth
    You are the sweetness
    That never runs out

    You are my first love
    You kissed my ears
    You spoke my name
    And calmed my fears

    You are my first love
    You kissed my feet
    You walked beside me
    On Emmaus street

    You are my last love
    You kissed my soul
    You dwell within me
    And make me whole

    You are my first love
    You are my last
    You're arms forever
    Will hold me fast

Listen

Listen to the beating waves
Pounding on the shore.
Listen to the crashing sound
Speaking o'er and o'er.

Listen to the tympani
Smoothing rock and rill.
Listen to the symphony
Echo through the hills.

Listen to the beating heart
Steady in the breast.
Listen to the pulsing surge
Pushing to the crest.

Listen to the faithfulness,
Constant to the call.
Listen to Emmanuel,
God is with us all.

May 1988
On the North Shore with my husband Tom and John Parkos

Advent
They That Wait Upon the Lord

Isaiah 40:31 "They that wait upon the Lord will renew there is strength, they will soar as with eagles wings; they will run and not grow weary, walk and not grow faint."

Advent is a time when the church celebrates the gift of waiting. Our twentieth century American culture needs this gift, of this discipline. We live in an instant gratification society with everything from instant food to instant cash. We naturally carry these habits and expectations into our life and find it difficult and frustrating to wait for anything, to say nothing about waiting for God's presence or direction.

I don't like to think of waiting as a passive experience because waiting is not doing nothing. I like to think about waiting in the context of a trip. For me, one of the best things about going on a trip, or on vacation, is the anticipation. I'm sure you have heard or said to yourself, "Half of the fun of going on a trip is getting ready." If I have been to a place before I can remember how much fun I had, who I saw, what I did and what I felt. If I haven't been there before I am excited about the unknown and unfamiliar.

Advent is a time of anticipation, a time of waiting. We remember what it must have been like when Joseph and Mary were waiting for Jesus to be born and we anticipate the second coming of Jesus. I want to learn to savor each time of waiting as a time to prepare my heart for the coming of Jesus. I want to be fully aware of the meaning that waiting has for me, of what it can teach me. I want to be aware of all of those who have no choice but to embrace or accept waiting. For the poor who must wait in line for their food and housing and medical care. For all of those in prison who are waiting for visitors or for their sentence to be up. For all of those who are hospitalized and are waiting to go home; to their families or to God. It is in the silent times that I begin to realize that all my life is a time of preparation for the coming of Jesus. Jesus is standing at the door of my heart waiting for me to open it so that He can come in and have supper with me.

In my time of meditation on waiting I remember another time in my life that taught me about waiting. Tom and I were expecting our first child. My due date was on Thanksgiving Day. Guess how long we had to wait? Ann Marie was born on Christmas Day. That wait, from Thanksgiving to Christmas was one of the longest I have experienced. I will always remember that Advent. God taught me a lot in that time of waiting. One of the things I learned was how impatient I am. Another was that the gifts God gives us are the most precious! Tom was laid off from his job and we didn't have any money for gifts, but God chose to give us a present that money could never buy – a beautiful little girl. I was beginning to understand the sacrament of waiting.

One of the things that waiting teaches me is silence. I am slowly learning the beauty and the power of being quiet. I am learning this in many ways. Throughout the years children have taught me a lot about many things, one of these is silence. I recall an incident that happened when Jennie, our youngest daughter, was seven years old. It was Thanksgiving night and I was tired so I went to bed early. Jennie crawled in with me to cuddle and to talk. She had missed her Grandma that day because Grandma had died the January before and this was the first Thanksgiving without her. Jennie started to cry and said through her tears, "I don't want you and Daddy to die." I tried to comfort her and told her how sad I was too, and I held her while we cried together. I said, "Let's listen to Jesus and hear what He has to say to us." We were just silent together for a while. After a time I asked her what Jesus was telling her? Jennie replied, "He said, 'Jennie, I love you very much and I won't leave you alone.'" She had a tiny smile on her face, and we held each other very tightly for a few more minutes. Then she said something that I never expected a seven-year-old to say. She said, "You sure have to respect silence, don't you Mom?"

God gave me a message through her that night. A message of how important it is to wait in silence, to listen to God and to let God love and heal me. I want to prepare for Christmas this year by respecting the gift of waiting. I want to experience waiting in a sacramental way, an outward sign of God's presence in my life.

Let us wait together this Advent. Let us learn to listen to what God wants to do with our lives. Let us anticipate the best trip we will ever have; the one that Jesus has planned for us and expects to go on with us. Thomas Merton said, "Make ready for the Christ whose smile, like lightening, sets free the song of everlasting glory that now sleeps in your paper flesh like dynamite."

Jesus has promised us that if we wait upon the Lord we will be renewed. Our strength will be renewed, and we will soar as with eagles 'wings. We will run and not grow weary we will walk and not grow faint. This is because we will be using God's power to love, forgive, heal and to build each other up. It is worth the wait!

Jesus was born for us, He lived for us, He died for us, and He rose from the dead for us. In actuality, we really don't have to wait for Him because He lives in our hearts by the consent we make to "live out" our baptism through the power of the Holy Spirit. Why do we celebrate Advent when we don't have to wait for God? I think it is because we need to learn about waiting, about patience and about silence. I know I need to do that. Let us remember that God is always waiting to be present to us and for us. Just as the first Christian Community waited together for the coming of the Holy Spirit at Pentecost, let us wait together for the coming of Jesus. Remember, half of the fun is getting ready.
Maranatha – Come Lord Jesus!

Morning Mist

The mist rose up with sun this morn -
Like incense in a giant bowl.
Ascending with my sunrise prayer,
Spreading fragrance everywhere.

The mist rose up with sun this morn –
Like smoke from smoldering fire.
Reflected in the glossy lake,
Natures' mirror makes no mistakes.

The mist rose up with sun this morn –
And walked upon the water.
She beckoned me to play the game
And waited there until I came.

June 1988

Evensong

The stars are in their bowl,
The chill is on its way,
The moon a crescent roll,
Lighting up the bay.

The leaves are standing still,
They listen to their breath.
The birds have stopped their trill,
And bow their heads to rest.

My heart is wide awake,
It pounds to let me know.
Love will never break,
Or ever let me go.

My soul will never know,
The setting of the sun.
Or see the dying glow,
Her day is never done.

June 1988

To an Autumn God

Strip my leaves that I may be
A barren tree in need of thee.

Let me see each leaf as pride,
Falling like the tears I cried.

Let me be a supple birch,
Stooping low to enter church.

Let your wind blow hard and strong,
Binding me where I belong.

Let me be a solid oak,
Planted by the stream of hope.

Let my limbs grow ever wide,
Holding all who come inside.

Strip my leaves that I may be,
Transparent and in love with thee.

September 1988

Silence is Golden

Silence is golden,
Like sun's brightest rays.
It shines from the inside
To light up the way.

Silence is golden,
A treasure to find.
So sell all your noises
And give it your mind.

Silence is golden,
Like trees in the fall.
It speaks without words
And hears when I call.

Silence is golden,
Like harvested wheat.
It comes in rejoicing
And brings in the sheaves.

Silence is golden,
Like moon in the dusk.
It's beauty no words
Could possibly touch.

Silence is golden,
And shouts to my heart.
Let love be the bonding
That sets us apart.

During retreat at Villa Maria

Here Comes My Bride

Here comes my bride,
Lovely in my eyes.
Carrying the cross,
Counting not the cost.

Here comes my bride,
Confident in stride.
Carrying my son,
Hidden holy one.

Here comes my bride,
Father at her side.
Carrying the dove,
Descended from above.

Here comes my bride,
Veiled but not disguised.
Carrying the crown
Flowers woven round.

Here comes my bride,
No blemish to hide.
Carrying the scroll,
Our names upon the roll.

Here comes my bride,
Radiant and alive.
Carrying the bouquet
She'll never throw away.

September 1988

Visitation

I went upon a journey
From head into my heart.
A thousand miles I wandered
And that was just the start.

I traveled from my mind to soul,
The road was long and steep.
And I, exhausted, lay upon
A shattered dream to sleep.

When I awoke in morning light
I turned around to see,
A lovely woman running fast
Her arms outstretched to me.

"You are my sister, you are my friend,
I came to be with you.
I am the mid-wife of a heart
That always will be true."

She stayed to watch and wait with me,
My time had now begun;
And we rejoiced to hear the cry
As I brought forth my son.

I'm still walking on the journey
From head into my heart;
But now I have companions
Whom even death can't part.

We praise, exult and bless God's name
We live where heart meets head;
The dwelling place of Jesus Christ
Who raised us from the dead.

November 1988

Presence

    I just want to be here
    Sitting down with you,
    Letting just your presence
    Be the stunning view.

    I just want to be here
    Speaking without words,
    Being without doing,
    Silence loudly heard.

    I just want to be here
    Looking in your eyes,
    Soul's mirror reflects in
    Beautiful disguise.

    I just want to be here
    With a smile and tear,
    Giving us a message,
    Love can hold no fear.

    I just want to be here
    Listening to your breath.
    Breathing in the fullness,
    Breathing out the death.

    I just want to be here
    With our God between,
    Leading us to lay down,
    By the quiet stream.

    I just want to be here
    In this dwelling place,
    Seeing loves' bright candles
    Shining in your face.

    I just want to be here
    For eternity.
    Heart to heart forever,
    One in you and me.

February 1989

Sisters Prayer

Let us sit with you and rest,
Let us lie against your breast.

Let us be your secret brides,
You, the cliff in which we hide.

Let us love you heart to heart,
Death will never set apart.

Let us look into your face,
Image of your loving grace.

Let us eat your risen bread,
Broken by the life you led.

Let us drink your precious wine,
Taken from the holy vine.

Let us be both food and drink,
For the cold and desolate.

Let us be a home for you,
Dwelling set apart from view.

Let us go with you to die,
In the cave with you to lie.

Let us rise on Easter morn,
From the tomb of self be born.

Let us know that now you live,
As your spirit to us give.

Let us share our life with these,
Committed to the God we please.

Let us go into the world,
With "I love you" as his words.

Let us join the holy throng,
Praising you from dawn to dawn.

March 1989

To Be

I want to be a running brook
Flowing free to thee.
Skipping over rocks and rills,
Running to the sea.

I want to be a flying bird
Riding on the breeze.
Playing in the sky,
Homing in the trees.

I want to be a graceful deer
Drinking from the lake.
Bowing head in prayer
Her communion takes.

I want to be a shining star
Hidden in the sun.
Twinkling in the sky
When the day is done.

I want to be a stately pine
Arms outstretched and raised,
Branches waving hands
In a song of praise.

I want to be a supple birch
Binding in the breeze,
Whispering "I love you"
To the other trees.

April 1989

Rain, Rain

Rain, rain, don't go away
I want to stay inside.
I don't want to go out to play
The game of seek and hide.

Rain, rain, don't go away
I listen to your sound
And know the tears of many years
Are watering my ground.

Rain, rain, don't go away
Stay and cry out your eyes.
Tomorrow is another day
The sun will dry your sky.

Rain, rain, don't go away
Just weep and let tears flow.
For what you feel is very real
God's Spirit has bestowed.

Rain, rain, don't go away
I'm sheltered from the wind.
Inside the arms that never harm
Just resting close to them.

June 1989
At Jim's cabin

Fecundity

Accept my seed oh fertile earth,
Softened by tears over many years.
Receive the child that I sowed in pain.
She is not afraid of the burial,
For she is prepared to die.

Grow strong, my seed, planted in the womb
Of my heart and nurtured through the night.
Wait in this time of concealment;
Do not be afraid of the dark.
Only there can you see my light.

Come forth, my seed, growing through the soil.
Push towards my son, the holy one;
Rejoice in this time of growth.
Do not be afraid of the passage
For life is not easily begun.

Bear fruit, my seed, in the autumn of your life.
Give me the yield from your field;
This is the time of harvesting.
Do not be afraid of loving
For in giving you will be healed.

September 1989
Written at Dunrovin and dedicated to my birthmother, Lois Hickok on her death, 10/23/1990

The Visit

It was a quiet night
And I was drawn to you
My silent friend,
To share your solitude.

It was a restless night
And I was drawn to you
My lovely friend,
To spend an hour or two.

It was a brilliant night
And I was drawn to you
My precious friend,
Jewel hidden from view.

It was a holy night
And I was drawn to you
By cords of perfect love,
And strands of gratitude.

September 1989
On retreat at Dunrovin

Adoration

When we gather please remember
That I want to be with you
I just want to sit and listen
To your heart beat strong and true

When we gather please remember
I have not forgotten you
I will never cease to ponder
On the beauty of my view

When we gather please remember
All of those who have no home
I will put them in my dwelling
So they will no longer roam

When we gather please remember
Those who lie upon their beds
You will visit them for me
Lay your hands upon their heads

When we gather please remember
I enjoy your company
We are bread and wine together
As you sacrifice for me

When we gather please remember
I will never leave you here
For our love must be outgoing
In the breaking, to be shared.

When we gather please remember
I'm in you and you in me
We will always be together
Pattern of the Trinity

December 1989
Dedicated to John Parkos on his 51st Birthday

Soldiers Field

    The hills show signs of spring
    The earth is turned again;
    Receiving sisters' seeds
    Who willingly agreed.

    Like army on parade
    Each stone is carefully laid,
    And as the day grows dim
    I see the saints come marching in.

    They have gone before
    To open up the door;
    To let our Savior in
    And drink the cup with Him.

    So let us visit them
    Amid triumphant hymn;
    And learn that faithfulness
    Is buried in the dust.

    And let us sing their song
    As women we belong;
    With all these holy ones
    We're sisters of God's son.

    This is the soldiers' field
    When love it's harvest yields,
    And those who gave their life
    Become the captain's wife.

March 1990
A meditation written while on retreat at Good Council in Mankato, praying in the Sisters of Notre Dame's cemetery.

The Lilies

    Turn up your face –
    I want to hold it in my hands
    Give me the flowers of your eyes
    Know I understand

    Turn up your face –
    I want to lose myself in you
    Give me the flowers of your eyes
    Do not deprive me of the view.

    Turn up your face –
    I want to look at me in you
    Give me the flowers of your eyes
    Our love has made us new

    Turn up your face –
    I want to meet your gaze
    Give me the flowers of your eyes
    Lilies of our resurrection days.

September 1989.
Another favorite poem written at Dunrovin; very healing for me.

The Lilies

Turn up your face —
I want to hold it in my hands.
Give me the flowers of your eyes
And know I understand.

Turn up your face —
I want to lose myself in you.
Give me the flowers of your eyes
Do not deprive me of the view.

Turn up your face —
I want to look at me in you.
Give me the flowers of your eyes;
For I have made you new.

Turn up your face —
I want to meet your gaze.
Give me the flowers of your eyes
Lilies of my Resurrection Days.

   Elizabeth Langlois

Waiting in May

It is May and we wait again
For spirit-wind to send the breeze
Blowing on my face;
Preliminary to embrace.

It is May and we wait again
For leaping flames of love to rest
Like hot tongues of fire;
Appeasing all of our desires.

It is May and we wait again
To hear that Mary's sent to visit
Another pregnant one;
Elizabeth, heavy with her son.

It is May and we wait again
For wind and flame, the Spirit to descend.
We who bear the Christ inside;
Are flowers for God's holy bride.

May 1990

Heartbroken

The lake was still and calm
    Until your wind
      Hit the sails of my heart
        And tore the jib apart.

June 1990

Unveiling

We talked together
  In the warmth of the day,
    With our hearts on fire
      Burning within our breasts -
        Together we entered God's rest.

When I heard you say "Eden"
  I remembered God's words,
    "It is not good for man to be alone -
      I will give him a woman to help him home."

When I heard you say Eden"
  I knew that you and I
    Were together in paradise -
      The veils lifted from our soul's disguise.

Friends Dialogue

Mary of Bethany
    After you have washed my feet with your tears
    After you have broken the jar of your fears
    After you have dried my feet with your hair
    After you have kissed them naked and bare
Jesus
    Then I will break my hearts disguise
    And kiss you with my gentle eyes
    Then pour the oil that never ends
    From the alabaster jar named friends

September 1990

Joyce Kilmer Revisited

    I think that I will never hear
        A poem as lovely as a deer;
        A silent statue in the glen
        With her children – guarding them.
    I think that I will never hear
        A poem as lovely to my ear;
        As robin, wren or whippoorwill
        Who wake me with their treble trills.
    I think that I will never hear
        A poem as lovely to be near;
        As you, whom God has given me
        To cherish for eternity.

                July 1991
                To Tom

Waves

This morning the lake was a still small voice -
Gentle lap of waves
Barely audible, but always beating
Like my heart, a mantra
Spoken in a whisper, always the same,
Breaking over the pain.

This afternoon the lake is a mighty roar –
A lion conquering lamb.
Loudly calling, breaking
Like my heart – a mantra
Spoken in a shout.

Life Goes On

Life goes on
    Is what you said
After you left
My heart disturbed
By your words
    That broke like bread

Life goes on
    But never the same
After your eyes
Told me your choice
After your voice
    That spoke my name

Life goes on
    I'll never forget
After our talk
Heart asunder
After thunder
    And no regrets

July 1991

Yes to No

I'm saying "yes" again
    To "no"
It's a little easier
Here by the shore
Of the lake;
Superior to all others.
Where the water is so clear
You can see to the bottom of
    It's soul.

I'm saying "yes" again
    To "no"
It's a little easier
By the water;
One of the great, where we make
Love that never ends
Like pounding waves crashing
Out of control.

July 1991

Sister Moon

My sister moon is rising
As full as she can be
And I am rising with her
Into eternity

My sister moon is shining
Reflections of the sun
She sends her healing light
To mend the broken ones

My sister moon is riding
Across the darkened sky
She watches o'er my sleeping
And comforts when I cry

My sister moon is calling
I hear her in the wind
She wants me to come out
To play with her again

My sister moon is setting
But she will come again
She is a true companion
An everlasting friend

Home

You are a little line
In the poems of God
The one that is written
By hand, from the heart
Of flesh, not of stone.
You are a sacred sonnet named home.

February 1992

Come Back

Come back to the time of greening - your youth;
Come back to the season of beauty and truth.

Come back to the time of dancing in fields,
And picking wild berries from God – given yield.

Come back to the summers when you were a girl,
And I was your champion with banners unfurled.

Come back to the day when my time and your own;
Were one heart pounding and we were at home.

Come back to the years when all time stood still,
And we played together - King of the Hill.

Come back to the woods where I took your hand;
And pledged allegiance to your lovely land.

Come back to the church we stood side by side;
I was the groom, and you were the bride.

Come back to the forest where we picked wildflowers;
I watched you paint them for hours and hours.

Come back to the night the moon was full gold;
We walked together down paradise road.

Come back to the hour when rain fell like tears,
And we knew our love would weather the years.

Come back to the memories were frozen in time;
Our love is eternal and wedding bells chime.

Come back to the greening –to the beautiful earth;
Drink deep of the water, rejoice in rebirth.

On retreat at Dunrovin; June 1992. Dedicated to our loving family on our 50th Wedding Anniversary May 11, 2007

Remember the Times

Remember the times of dreaming the dreams
When all of the world was enchanted
With stories of old.
You were aware
That you were listening to them;
The ones begun with "once upon a time",
And you knew that you were part of the rhyme.
+
Remember the times of innocence
When all of the world was alive
With the sounds of life.
You were aware
That you were singing with them
The song that begins with "yes"; and
You were dancing in your wedding dress.
+
Remember the times of passion
When all of the world was aflame
With color filled words.
And you were aware
That you were feeling desire;
Then all of the stories and all of the songs
Became all of the places where you belonged.

June 1992
On retreat at Dunrovin
Dedicated to Aimee on her wedding day 9-17-1995
Ann on her wedding day 9-7-2002
Brynn on her wedding day 8-14-2015
Claire on her wedding day 10-7-2017
Natasha on her wedding day 6-22-2018
Amanda on her wedding day 10-13-2018
Andrew on his wedding day 8-29-2020

Free Verse

    This I will never give up –
    The living of life and the loving
    The agony and the ecstasy
    I was not living before
    I met you.
    Only breathing a shallow breath
    Barely enough to stay alive,
    Barely enough to say yes
    To another day,
    To this new way.

    This I will never give up –
    The pain and the joy of loving
    For now I am no longer dead
    And buried alive,
    But alive and buried
    In the haven of your heart,
    Fully breathing in the life
    Fully breathing out the death.
    Knowing I love you and you love me
    Gives life and endless energy.

June 1992

3
Poems From My Sixties

Garden

Last night my sister moon
Made me a lovely path across the lake
And I walked on the water
To a place where
I thought I had never been.
But, when I looked around
I knew I had been there before
And my dream was not a dream anymore.

She took me through a gate
That was opened, full ajar
And in the brilliant moon light
I saw a garden there.
The flowers nodded welcome
Their fragrance filled my soul;
In this sacred place
God's healing was bestowed.

I'll never leave this garden
It lives within my heart;
The rivers always flowing
Their waters never part.
I'll go there when the moon
Makes a path across the sea;
And lights for me the way
To the secret garden I named love.

March 1993
My 60th Birthday

Kataluma

I am at home.
Here in my hermitage
Like cocoon in the woods
I am protected,
Aware that this is Kataluma
A place where I can rest,
A place to put my burdens down,
A place to be, to be me, to be freed.
An inn, where there is room
To cry, to die, to rise,
To sing, to lay, to fly on wings
Of wild imaginings.

I am a monarch now,
Landing on the flowers
Of faith, of hope, of love.
I drink deeply and pleasure in
Bright spring blossoms;
The trinities of trillium,
Yellow marsh marigolds,
Purple violets, hidden in leaves of green
(I saw more than I had ever seen).

This I know,
They are waiting patiently
Their smiling faces to show,
In this Kataluma place there is
A flaming flower named Rose.
Sleeping under blanket white, she too grows,
Waiting for the Easter winds to rush
And melt the snow.

March 1993

When You are Gone

How can I not miss you?
You, whom I hold in my heart
So very often
More than I care to admit
I admit to care
Yes – I dare.

September 1993

Twins

I see you now my lovely lady lake –
You played hide-n-seek all summer.
With the leaves fully green
You could barely be seen.
But now the birch are bare.
Autumn cut their hair
And you can no longer hide.
I gaze at you;
Blue, brilliant, brightly beautiful.
I love your naked form,
The way you let Spirit Wind
Lead you in the dance.
The sun and moon upon your face,
The pounding of your heart.
As we look at one another
We can't tell each other apart.

November 1993
On Lake Superior. She is definitely a muse, as well as having a twin sister.

Underground

I just haven't been able to write;
Words that like a river flowed
Seem frozen under the ice and snow.
They don't ripple across the water of my mind,
They don't dance in the sunlight of my soul,
Or speak in the deep pool of my heart.
So, I sit quietly in the dark
Remembering the ripples, the dance, the sounds,
For only a season run underground.

January 1994
Pecos, New Mexico

Dare

I admit to the bond
The cord of love between us
Unseen but not unreal.
Woven on the loom of faith,
Woven with a warp of forgiveness,
Woven with the woof of fidelity,
Woven together with all we love,
Making a colorful garment of praise.
I am amazed!!

Silence Speaks
Don't cut me with a knife
Just leave me on the plate
And eat me by hand a little at a time.
I will fill you with satisfaction
For I long to be your friend –
To sit in your presence
So we can breathe together
The pure clean air of communion
On the mountain of reunion.

March 1994

Pecos River Reflection

Why do rivers fascinate me so?
Where do they come from, where do they go?
What do they carry that illuminates my soul?

I think they speak to me of death
Of floods and fight for life,
And overflow and sinking boats
Colliding in the night.

I think they speak to me of life
Of source and running free,
And merging of the little streams
To form community.

I think they speak of me to you
And what you mean to me.
God's gracious gift running through my heart,
Friends through eternity.

January 1994

Grief

This pain I hold
    Tenderly and with much respect
    Like a friend
    Who came in from the cold
    Like a treasure of old gold
    That I found on the road.

My arms encircle and embrace
    This deep ache
    She will never go away
    For I will preserve her
    With the salt of my tears
    And the passing of years.

I brought her forth from my broken heart
    And nurtured her under my breast.
    She sits on my knee where we both agree
    That love and pain go together –
    You can't have one without the other.

March 1994
To Aimee

Here and Now

This is a bittersweet time
Like the kind
You picked near the Villa
And wouldn't tell me
Where you found it.

I was asking where
For a long, long time,
Now I only ask why,
In this bittersweet time
Of your good-bye.

This is a bittersweet time
Like the kind
You put on the altar
Next to the small wooden plate
Holding Eucharist.

I was asking why
For a long, long time,
But now I only ask how,
In this bittersweet time
Of here and now.

April 1994

Samaritan Woman

The well is deep
I saw it from afar
And thought it mirage
But as I came with my jar
I knew my eyes
Had not been fooled
And in the middle of the desert
There was a living pool.

I lowered the bucket
To the bottom
Where clear, clean water flows
And just as I was about to leave
I met this beautiful man.
I knew his eyes had not been fooled
They looked in mine with love
And filled my empty pool.

He told me
All about who I was
And with whom I had been.
He was telling me more
Than words can ever speak.
I knew my heart had not been fooled
So I ran to tell others
About Jesus and the healing pool.

May 1994

Mandorla*

I have gone into the forest,
The woods of my soul
Where the trees grow tall
And the flowers are wild like me.
The only way I can find the path
Is by keeping my eyes on the sun by day
And on the moon by night.
The forest is a place of solitude.
It is here in my aloneness
That I find my at-homeness.
It is here that the beasts
Clamor for my attention.
I listen to each one
And as I call them by name –
They become tame.
I embrace the demons and the divine –
They are both mine.
Here the lion and the lamb
Lie down beside the
Still waters of my soul.
This is the place of Mandorla
Where all become whole;
The sacred space where opposites embrace,
Where God and Goddess stand face to face.

May 1994

Silence

Silence is the loudest sound of love
For it shouts without words
What the heart heard.
Let us share this silent space
And make *Mandorla in the sacred place.
Together we will hear the silent sounds;
Take off your shoes, we stand on holy ground.

September 1994

*Mandorla is a symbol of bringing together opposites and represents the place where opposites come together to create wholeness.

The Storm

> I listen to the gentle sound,
> Water on the roof and ground.
> Tears reflecting all the pain
> Like the clouds of pouring rain.
>
> I am crying like the sky
> And listening to it's lullaby,
> Rocking me to restless sleep
> While outside it continues to weep.
>
> When I awake the rain has stopped
> But in my soul the tears still drop.
> Now, I'll put on my smile again
> Covering the storm within.
>
> *June 1994*

To John

> How fitting that the hall is bare
> With no pictures hanging there.
> Nothing but the nails are left
> And memories of happiness.
>
> *June 1994*

Prayer While Watching the Ice Go Out

> Let the ice go out in my heart O God
> Unthaw the surface of my lake.
> Move across the waters of my soul
> That I may be able to plumb the depths.
> Be a deep-sea diver in me and
> Catch the pearls of great price
> Hidden in my shell – make me well.
>
> *April 1996*

Eve of Pentecost

Spring, are you waiting for me this year?
I feel like I don't have to catch up with you;
Like you are very patient with me
While I linger in the tomb.
You are so aware that I'm not a forced bloom.
So aware of the Kairos moment
Soon I'll be walking outside in the garden.
Already I can smell the flowers
And hear the birds singing.

Come and take my hand;
   I'm ready to go outside to play
   I'm ready to see your beauty and mine.
     Some things cannot be done alone –
(The tomb was certainly a place to discover that!)

My desire for you is rising like the sap
     Running in the maples
My desire for you is as powerful as the
     Wild water running down the river
My desire for you is hidden in the woods
     Of my heart, like the violet it is shy.
     The only thing I never ask is why.

May 1996

Dawn

The morning dove is cooing
The robin trilling sweet.
The cardinal is singing
The raven couple greets.
They make a lovely setting for night and day to meet.
The birds are greeting the dawn and a beautiful crescent
Moon is hanging on the eastern wall of the sky.

July 1996

Olympic Opening 1996

You each arrived from your own little world,
With your own little tales of triumph.
Each face shining, brilliant,
Eyes dancing with excitement.
Your names were placed in the record book,
Bound together with a common purpose.
You carry our world in the palms of your hands.

You carry the hopes and the dreams,
You carry the winning and losing,
You carry your future within you.
You carry the stories you'll tell
About running the race and fighting the fight.

So -
Carry the torch for all of us,
Carry the banners high!
We are all sisters and brothers –
Don't let the journey die!

July 1996

Winter

Winter	Never arrives gradually
	One day at a time
No	It is here in the sudden storm
	In the twinkling of an eye
I	Watch from the window
	As the snow soundlessly descends
Soon	The children will be playing in it
	Excited by the joy of its newness
Winter	Runs to greet us with abandon
	But I am slow to embrace it

Where is the child in me?

Canticle

My heart has ever been ready for you.
It lay broken in my breast yet no more stone-like,
It was now made of flesh.
Softened by my tears, by the years,
Softened by the pain of patience.
Learning that love must wait
Like winter waiting to pass,
Like good wine saved for last.
+
Come, my friend, the mate of my soul;
You touched me and made me whole.
Listen to the beating of our heart-clocks
Ticking out beyond the reason for anything.
When has love ever been reasonable?
+
I remember they said it would not last.
I heard you laugh and now it's half-past.
Have past light and night draws nigh.
Do I hear you cry? Do I hear you sigh?
+
Come, my beloved, I'll dry your eyes.
Open the gate, its late and our bed awaits.
We are among the chosen few;
My heart has ever been ready for you.

May 1997
To Tom on our 40th Wedding Anniversary

Words

    I've been afraid to write.
    The words are so deeply buried.
    Without them I would perish.
    Will they still exist once spoken?
    Will they vanish like vapor from my breath?
    It seems impossible to dig them up;
    The ground is so hard, and I've lost my shovel.
    They are the precious prize won in my
    Struggle to become a lover.
    I'm so afraid to tell you what they are;
    I hold them under the cover of my heart,
    Like a blanket to insulate against the cold.
    They keep me warm inside
    Where they need no disguise.
    Only a glance from your eyes
    That say, "My Beloved".

February 1997

Common Ground

    I came in pain and joy,
    Grasping one in each hand,
    Holding them tightly in my heart.
    Then I was held up
    By the bandit God;
    "Lift up your arms" s/he said.
    "Open your hands" God said,
    Then this bandit God
    Caught the pain and the joy,
    Mixed them together in a cup
    And lifted it to my lips.
    As I drank I knew
    I could hold them both
    In the place of common ground.
    Where everything whole is found and
    All opposites are held;
    The chalice of my heart.

January 1998
Published in Richard Rohr's newsletter after the Common Ground retreat

Going to Kosovo

My prayers are full of people
Faces of my sisters and brothers
I see them and weep for
I know they are me
And I am them
We are one
I have never known their suffering but
Whatever I have known unites us
They are fleeing their homes
Hatred has driven them out
Another Herod is killing the innocents
They carry their babies in weary arms
Their old and worn-out carts
Like refuse these refugees from Kosovo
They don't know where they are going
My soul is aching with them
My heart is breaking for them
A small dark girl with a lovely smile
Holds up her only possession
A doll wrapped in a scrap of cloth
I wonder if her name is Elizabeth

April 1999

Mountain Place

I, in the valley of despair,
Turn to the God of mountain air,
Where all is pure and very rare,
So beautiful beyond compare.

+

When God who gives this mountain place,
Brings me to the stream of grace,
And as I bow my head to taste,
God gently gives me an embrace.

April 1999
To Mary Asher on her Birthday and to my twin sister Louise on our Birthday

Question

    Where have all the poems gone?
       Not a writer's block but heart is closed.
         Unwind my tightened clock
            Within this rigid body-block.
               So that my pen can flow again.

March 2000
Before myofascial release with Jerry Meyer

And I Was Loved

My body, tight and terrified –
Bending under the weight of the world.
She spoke to me in pain and wisdom
She told me her story and I cried.
The tears softened my cheeks and my heart.

They became diamonds, priceless treasures
After this rain, the sun was never more beautiful.
After this rain, the moon glowed from above
And I was loved.

April 2000
After bodywork with Jerry Meyer

Surprise Visit

    My heart is opening
        Like a door opens
             To greet a beautiful face
                On the other side
                    A person I love
                         Coming to visit

    I am very surprised
        When whom I see
             Standing on the threshold
                Pausing at the door
                    Is my very own self,
                      The one I call me.

October 2000

Open Eye Meditation

I see the light, your essence,
Shining out from the beacons of your eyes.

Shining out for:
    Those who are lost at sea and
    Looking for a safe harbor
    A place of calm and serenity
    A place of refuge and rest
    A place to drop their anchors of pain
    A place of healing where nothing
    Will ever be the same.

And now:
    I see the same light and essence
    Shining out from the beacons of their eyes.

Shining out for
    Others who are lost at sea
    Others who want to be free
    From all the restrictions that bind
    From all the fear that blinds
    From all the pain inside
    Others who are looking for a safe place
    Where acceptance is the space
    And touch the grace.

Caution!!!
    All of this shining is very contagious.
    Beaming out from the One who created us.

So:
    Open your eyes and look into mine
    And we'll give each other a beacon
    To shine.

October 2000

March Madness

March is hanging onto winter –
She doesn't want to let her go.
There is so much beauty
In the softly falling snow.

March is hanging onto winter –
Like leaves that cling to a tree.
She wants to keep her season
Instead of being free.

March is hanging onto winter –
Like my heart hangs onto you.
She doesn't remember that she surrenders
Spring will heal and renew.

March 2001
At Dwelling in the Woods

Eagles

Eagles in flight,
Such a beautiful sight.
They catch an air wave
And glide without effort;
Like surfers letting the water take them
To the shore and then go back for more.
Like a leaf in the river of life –
Going with the flow – letting go.

May 2002

Trilogy on Grief

Skygrief

The sky has been crying all night.
I know the feeling and it doesn't help to ask why.
How else can she shed her skin?
How else can she renew?
How else can she tell us that
No one was there to hold her hand?
Rain-tears water the parched land.

I have been crying all night too.
I'm happy for the healing tears bring.
Softening my heart like the rains of spring.
How else can the pain be released
Unless I learn the language of grief?

August 2001

Mornings' Sunrise

This mornings' sunrise
    Was wild and passionate.
Grandmother Moon,
    A silver bowl, surrounded by an
    Aura of gold, was patiently waiting
    To see the brilliant colors
    Flooding the sky and the lake.
Then slowly fading I knew she had not died –
    She was only hiding in the morning sky.

January 2002

Lost and Found

Love is never lost; it may be hidden or broken.
It may seem totally dead.
But, in the heart lies dormant a power that never ends.
So, let the tears flow freely,
Let the river flow.
Let your love be found
Under the melting snow.

March 2002

Dedicated to Elizabeth Rose Kuhne
Born 2-23-1960 Died 7-8-2002

4
Poems From My Seventies

Thou

I'm in another land,
The colors are vivid and bright;
I never see just black and white.
It's here I have learned that
Love is stronger than fear
And life is stronger each year.
It is here in the "Land of Now"
Where everything and everyone
Is Thou.

November 2002

70th Birthday Thoughts

This morning I arrive at five
I need some time to "be".
Before the day is wide awake,
Before the night goes to sleep,
Before the world comes alive.

Today is not a normal day
But I'm doing the ordinary things.
I make some coffee,
I light my oil lamp and incense,
I sit in my usual chair to pray.

Today I celebrate my birth.
I rejoice in the life given to me,
In the beauty of this earth.
I rejoice in the life given to me,
I celebrate the joy and tears.

Everything has been worth the cost
Of living all these years.

March 2003

Mary of Magdala

Remember me, I am with you.
I am here today
I wear a scarlet veil
Not a letter.
I wear the color red
That you may be fed
With the passion of my life.
With the truth that sets us free
To be woman of integrity.

June 2003
Written at "The Three Faces of Mary" Seminar at St. Catherine's University in St Paul, MN

The Poems

The poems I read early this morning
Woke me up!
They opened my heart to believe
That I was a part of everyone.
Yes, I was hidden in each line.
    I was a part of every rhyme.
    I was present in every poet.
How beautiful to know it!

July 2003
At Ravenrest

Mary Oliver says that the poem is not the world. It isn't even the first page of the world. The poem wants to bloom, like a flower – it knows that much. It wants to open itself, like the door of a little temple, so that you might step inside to be cooled and refreshed. Less yourself than part of everything.

Lectio Divine

I paused before opening the door.
The knock was faint, but persistent.
I stopped to listen –
This was risky business.
Who was there?
What did I have to fear?

Am I in danger?
Is this a stranger?
In my soul, as faint as the knock
I heard, "Open for I am the Word".
Yes, you do not need to fear,
Yes, you do need to hear,
Yes, you are in danger,
Yes, I am a stranger.
The choice is yours, it's up to you
If you open up you're among the few.

When I pushed open my door
The words came walking in
And marched into my heart.
Then I knew that they were a part
Of whom I was from the beginning of time.
Come to the waters, you who have no money, come.
Eat rich food and drink my cup.
This is the fare that fills you up.

January 2005

Initiation

When you return to earth Grandfather Sun will meet your dawn
And you will ride with him
Across the sky of your day
Until the night comes
And puts you to sleep
Under the stars where you lay.

When you return to earth Grandmother Moon will be there
To greet you and hold you
As you rest in the curve of her arm
All of the stars will know your
Constellation by name and the
Planets protect you from harm.

When you return to earth the garden will await your joy
And you will know your name
And the names of all the flowers,
Trees, birds and beasts
The ground will welcome your feet
AND PROTECT YOU FROM FAME!

September 2005
Written when my husband, Tom was making his "Rite of Passage" at Ghost Ranch, New Mexico with Fr. Richard Rohr

Wild Child
(to Jennie with a warning to Denny)

The years have passed so fast
Since the day you were born.
It was in early April
But the leaves had already
Come out of their wombs
And the world looked shiny new – Like you.

Morning had broken like the
Water that helped to
Bring you into my arms
Without harm.

As I held you for the first time
I knew that love is born again
With each child.
I listened to your cry
And broke into a smile;
This little girl would
Not be meek and mild –
I'm glad she sounds
A little wild!!

October 2005
For my daughter Jennie on her wedding day

Christmas Message

May you remember
    The peace you felt
When your Mother held you
    On her breast
And all you had to
    Do was rest.

December 2005

Love Signs

I know Christ wants us to be sacrament to each other
We see and feel and touch, become the outward sign.
This seemed impossible to me, that we are God's love.
I asked, "How can this be?"
God answered, "I use bread and wine then
Why not you to be me?"

I know Jesus used ordinary things to
Reveal that He was love.
The cleansing water flowing free
Oil that won't wash away
The salt which puckers baby's lips
Persevering vows just made.

So God uses you and me to witness Her love,
And slowly changes all of us into
Her body and blood.
Our fellowship a sign to those
Who do not know our Brother;
They see our friendship in the Lord and
How we love each other.

July 2007
Dedicated to the people of St Gregory's on our retirement

Mother God

Enough is never enough with God;
Abundance is Her second name
Excess Her first.
You know how She feeds the birds
And how the field lilies grow.
Without the toil, without the work,
You know how She clothes the earth
And throws caution to the wind.
God never has a little fling.

Thanksgiving, 2007

Unwritten Poetry

Nothing satisfies when poetry is denied;
Nothing but the bloody dawn.
The purple pink of nature's ink
Spread across the liquid lake.
Nothing but our meeting eyes,
When love is not disguised;
But boldly painted on your face
And felt within your warm embrace.

March 2008
Written at Ravenrest. Dedicated to Aimee on her 49th Birthday and to my dear husband Tom on his 79th Birthday

Heart Space

Trust in me with all your heart
Welcome me with all your heart
Receive me with all your heart
Love me with all your heart

I trust you with all my heart
I come to you with all my heart
I receive you with all my heart
I love you with all my heart

When you look in the mirror you see me –
When I look in the mirror I see you
When our eyes kiss we recognize each other
With our hands together we bow and say –
Namaste

August 2008

Everything Belongs

When I was a child
I lived in a house surrounded by a garden
My father tended the flowers,
My mother the fruit.

I loved to play in the garden,
To smell the flowers and learn their names
To touch the fruit and do the same.
I delighted in the garden,
The garden delighted in me.

When I became a young girl
I was given permission to pick a bouquet
To gather the fruit.
I loved to arrange the flowers in a vase
Look into each face.
Picking the fruit was more difficult
Especially the raspberries,
I picked, so I could eat.

When I brought the fruit and flowers inside
I realized how much pleasure they gave.
The fruit was tasty and sweet –
The flowers brightened our table.
God spoke to me through them;
"Bring my world inside.
Experience the beauty and the beast.
Know I dwell within the best and beast
Because everything belongs."

March 2009
Dedicated to Richard Rohr on my 76th Birthday

To Peggy Thompson

"Just let it flow –
Let it go wherever it wants to"
The paint is not easy to control
And I'm unable to cover mistakes.
Teaching me a lot about myself:
The background must be light
And then we all add layers –
More water, salt for the texture or tears;
A little darker paint each time
Letting it speak for itself.
The language of imagination and
Letting go of agitation;
Peaceful, just in the process.

October 2008
Creativity and Spirituality Retreat at St John's University led by Peggy Thompson

Palm Sunday

With joyful song amid the throng
We gather to hear the story.
We walk together, asking to be remembered.
We carry the Palms, then bring them home.
Bear witness of where we have been,
And where we are going
Knowing now why this day we can say
Is different from all others!!!

April 2011
Our first Palm Sunday at St Paul's Monastery

North Shore Morning

I slept very little last night
Knowing that the dawn wanted me
To see her beautiful face
Rising over the lake.

Brother Sun is now way over to the northeast
And Grandmother Moon is a slice of pie
Watching me in the southern sky.

A jet is writing a long white line between them;
Marking day and night in the planes straight flight.
As the night says goodbye to the day
I continue to praise and pray.

June 2012

Dawn with Psalm 19 at Ravenrest

The trees are meditating, so still, not moving.
The birds are chanting their mantras.
The Sun is showing up;
Painting a luminous path of gold;
Shouting "awake" across the sleepy lake.
A psalm of praise to the One
Who imagined all of this into existence.
Now, the handsome groom kisses his bride.
The beautiful one who smiles and says –
"Good morning my love, I am so happy to
Be here with you. Let us praise our maker
And declare in the beginning the words
That we promise together, FOREVER.

Autumn, 2012

Dedicated to my husband Tom who was the REAL BEST MAN on our wedding day May 11, 1957, and to our grandson Nicholas and his beautiful Bride Brynn on their wedding day August 14, 2015.

Easter 2012

Today I will feed myself with poetry
Why else would I want to want to get out of bed?
It's April and the rain is falling.
The desert is blooming and
May is close on my heels.
The taste of Rumi will remind me
Alone.
How delicious you are
How sweet to sit at your feet.
Flowers are coming out of their shells;
Their fragrance fills the air.
The Friend of my Heart, the Beloved,
Is standing by my side – He is alive!

April 2012

5
Poems from my Eighties

At the Monastery

I like to sit on the bench by the main door,
Next to the Jade Tree.
Her ancient leaves are thick and shiny;
She helps me to feel younger than I am.
Ready for the days that fill the present
And all of the tasks of a lifetime.

She says to me, "Just sit here and
Enjoy all of the memories,
Even the ones you want to forget.
They filled your life with the need for justice,
Tempered by the love that brought you here to reflect
On the common life we both long for,
As you sit on the bench by the main door."

June 2013
Written while attending the Sister's Retreat given by Sister
Christine Vladimiroff at St. Paul Monastery

Winter Rest

I feel so blessed
To have a place to sit and rest –
Just to watch the fire.
The woodpecker eating suet
The chickadees flying to & fro,
The trees laden down by snow –
Holding it in their branches
Until the wind blows it away.

As I meditate and pray
The very same thing happens to me.
All I have been holding
Is blown out of my tree
By the Spirit of Love
Who blows where she wills.
I just sit quiet and still
And feel so blessed
To have a place to sit and rest.

2013

Now

I am beginning to accept my eighties
It has taken me awhile.
There are so many unanswered questions,
So much I want to do that will remain undone.
It is years now since I celebrated my sixtieth birthday.
I've felt so many different emotions;
Joy, sadness, grief, fear, uncertainty,
Love and hope.

Now I'm much more serene and at peace.
Acceptance is the key to serenity –
I taste, touch and feel each moment.
My memories are jewels set out on a
Crystal plate.

They catch the sun and shine in the dark.
They are precious stones, but
Among them all there is one most precious.
It is the pearl of greatest price
I name it "now".

Each day I add more jewels to
That overflowing plate because I
Have to love what is right before me
And know it's never too late.

Blessed

How can we count the ways?
How can we count the days?
Our hearts so full of all the
Ways we have been blessed.
So much love pouring into them
By you our very beautiful daughter and friend.

December 2017
To Ann on her 60th Birthday

About the Author

Elizabeth Langlois was a wife, mother, sister and friend. She was also a spiritual guide, psychiatric nurse and counselor who had a deep desire to know God and express herself through her poems. She found her voice as a poet in her forties and was a prolific writer. She felt others' suffering deeply and throughout her life she fought for justice. Elizabeth's poems have touched those close to her and the hope is to share her wisdom, insight and inspiration with the world.

www.ingramcontent.com/pod-product-compliance
Lightning Source LLC
LaVergne TN
LVHW091545070526
838199LV00002B/212